Fun with Bl

MW01065199

Dona Herweck Rice

Publishing Credits

Rachelle Cracchiolo, M.S.Ed., *Publisher*
Conni Medina, M.A.Ed., *Managing Editor*
Nika Fabienke, Ed.D., *Content Director*
Véronique Bos, *Creative Director*
Shaun N. Bernadou, *Art Director*
Valerie Morales, *Associate Editor*
John Leach, *Assistant Editor*
Courtney Roberson, *Senior Graphic Designer*

Image Credits: p.2 (top), p.11 (top) Ron Fabienke; all other images from iStock and/or Shutterstock.

Teacher Created Materials
5301 Oceanus Drive
Huntington Beach, CA 92649-1030
www.tcmpub.com
ISBN 978-1-4938-9834-3
© 2019 Teacher Created Materials, Inc.
Printed in China
Nordica.082018.CA21800936

She would like to

make a .

robot

She would like to

make a .

castle

She would like to

make a .

plane

She would like to

make a  .

car

She would like to

make a .

rainbow

She would like to

make a  .

fish

She would like to

make a .

dog

She would like to

make a  .

heart

She would like to

make a .

tower

She would like to

make a .

bridge

High-Frequency Words

New Words

like   make

she   would

Review Words

a   to